# Starter Book 2

## The tunes in Level 1 used these sounds

These are the fingerings you used to play them

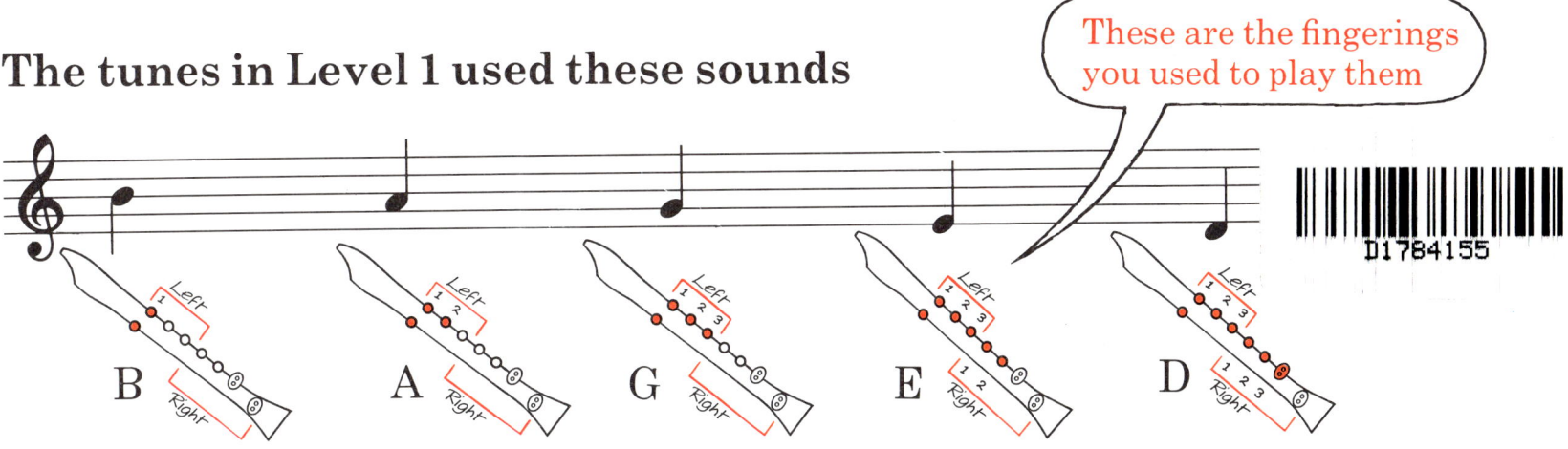

B  A  G  E  D

---

### The tunes in $\frac{2}{4}$ $\frac{3}{4}$ and $\frac{4}{4}$ used

walking notes
or crotchets
lasting 1 beat

running notes
or quavers lasting
$\frac{1}{2}$ beat each

crotchet rests
for
1 beat silence

### The tunes in $\frac{6}{8}$ used

step-skip beats
made up of
a crotchet
and a quaver

or steps
made up of
a crotchet
with a quaver rest

# Slurs and sirens

Pick me up with both hands.
Cover the thumb-hole,
and three finger-holes with **each** hand,
ready to play the note D.
Remember, left hand nearest my lip and yours.
Now blow through me a smooth and long
toooooooooooooooooooooooooooooooooooooo
Keep the tone steady.

Now blow again, only this time
lift your **right-hand first finger** on and off its hole,
making a sound like a siren.

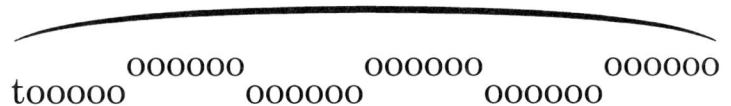

```
            oooooo       oooooo        oooooo
   tooooo          oooooo        oooooo
```

Notice you only say 't', or tongue, at the start of the sound.

When you join up notes like this you **slur** them.
The sound you joined with D was **F sharp**.

To play F sharp, cover the holes as for the note D but lift up the first finger of the right hand, like this:

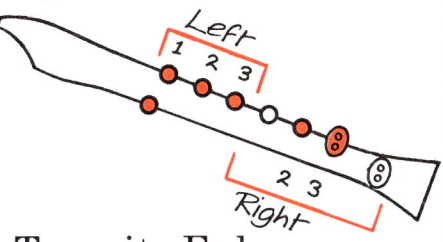

To write F sharp, put a note in the bottom space and write a sharp sign in front of it:

# Slur Mix

Just like D and F♯, other sounds can be tongued or slurred

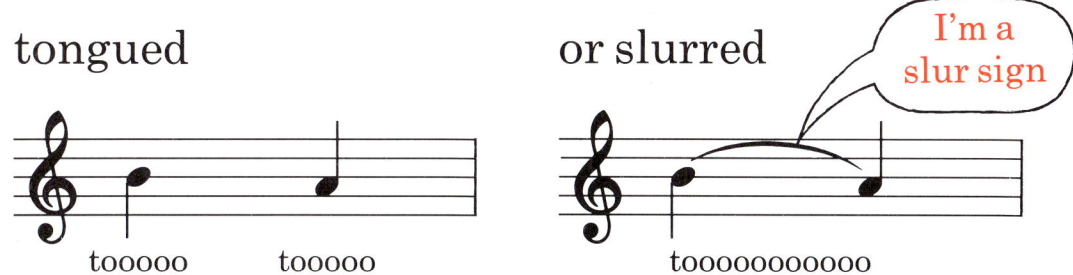

Here are some more groups to tongue or slur

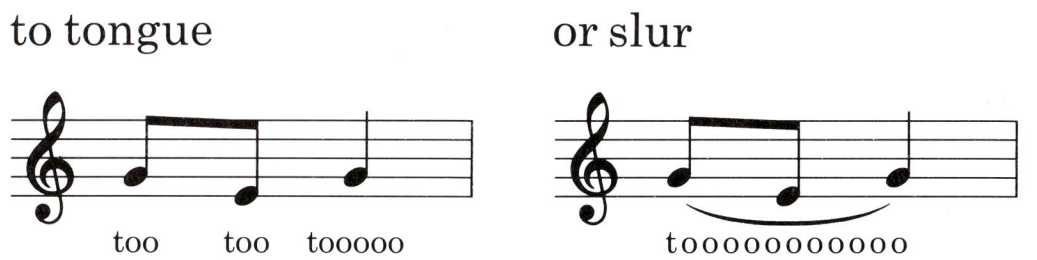

Mix them together to make tunes like this:

# On my hat

On my hat__ I once sat__

It was flat__ like a mat.

So for hat__ that was that.

Tunes with F♯ often end on G. They are in the key of G.

To show this, a sharp sign is written on the top line of the stave, like this:

This is called a key signature.

The top line of the stave is also F.

# Au clair de la lune

French traditional tune

# There's a hole in my bucket

# We've got a wheeliebin

We've got a wheel-ie - bin, a wheel-ie - bin, a wheel-ie - bin,

We've got a wheel-ie - bin, to put our rub - bish in.

Based on the traditional British tune 'Dance to Your Daddy'

7

# C′

To play top C,
(which we label C′),
cover the thumb-hole,
and the second hole,
like this:

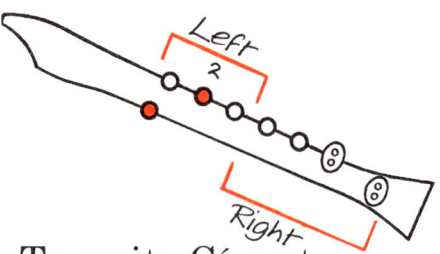

To write C′, put
a note in the space
above the middle line,
like this:

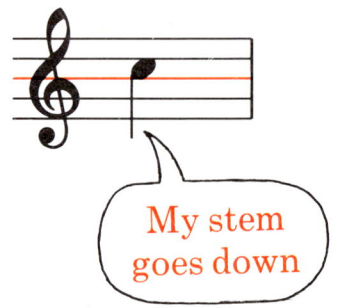

My stem goes down

## Word Mix

Can you remember the B A G tune
and the E G G tune?
Here they are:

Now that you know some more notes
you will be able to think up other 'word tunes'
to mix together.

Here are some ideas to get you going:

F A C E

C A G E

And some other words to turn into music:

BAGGAGE  FEED  CAFE  CADGE  BEEF

8

# Pease pudding hot

Traditional English

Pease pud-ding hot,    Pease pud-ding cold,

Pease pud-ding in the pot,    Nine days old.

# I like baked beans

I    like  baked beans    best   of   all.

That's  the   rea - son   I'm  so  tall.

# Hush little baby

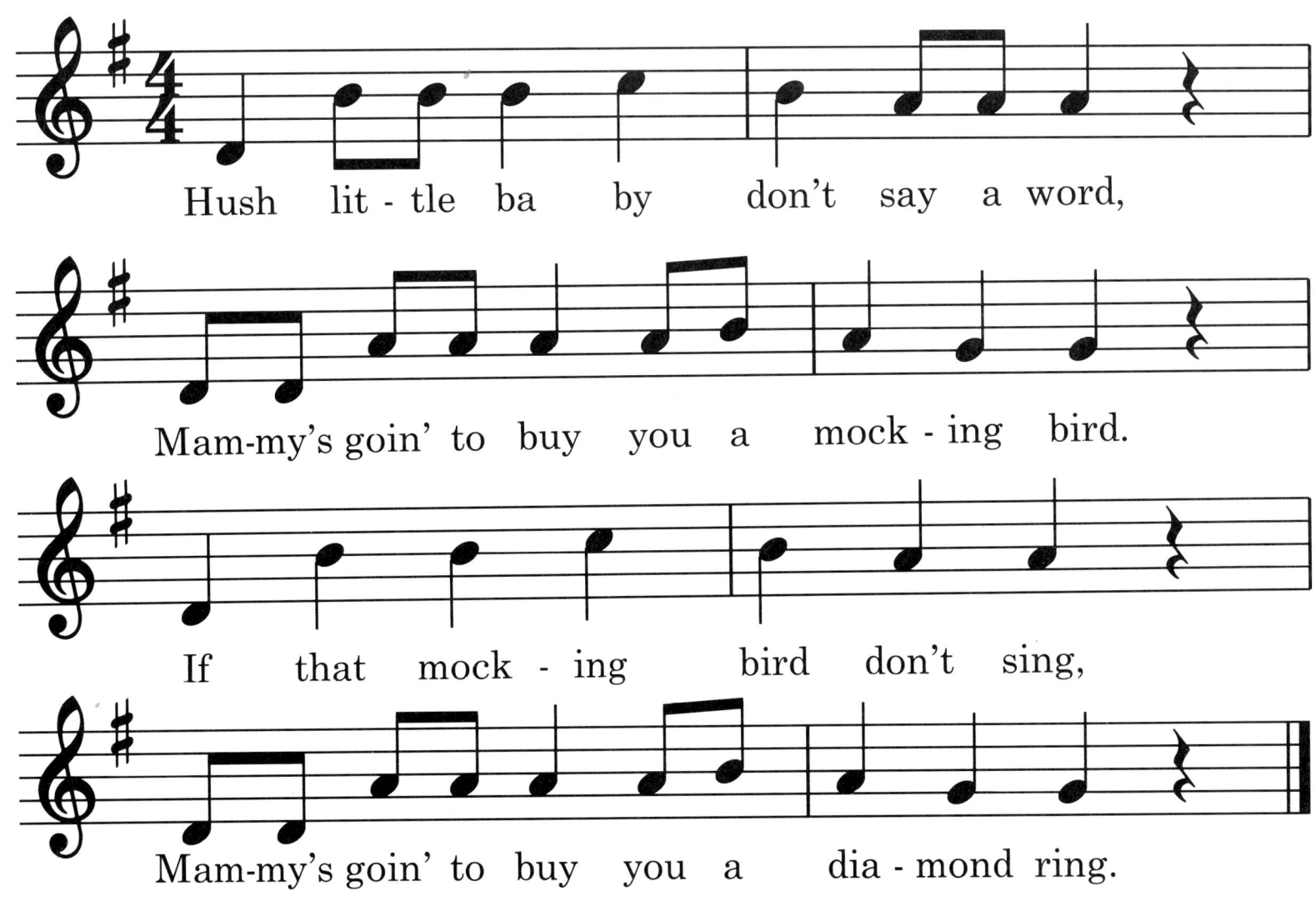

Hush lit - tle ba by don't say a word,

Mam-my's goin' to buy you a mock - ing bird.

If that mock - ing bird don't sing,

Mam-my's goin' to buy you a dia - mond ring.

Traditional American

10

# The CABBAGE Patch

How many cabbages are there in this patch?

## D′

To play top D
(which we label D′),
finger the note C′,
and then lift off
the thumb at the back,
like this:

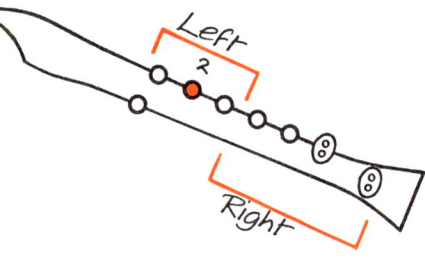

To write D′, put
a note on the fourth
line up, like this:

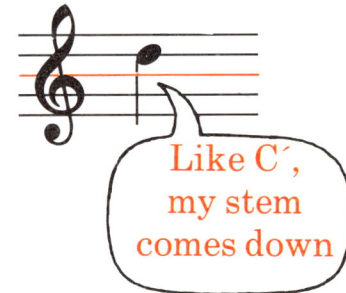

Like C′,
my stem
comes down

# Snakes and Ladders Mix

Here is a musical
ladder from G to D′.
Play up it a step
at a time:

Here is another ladder
from D to A:

Mix these ladders with little snakes

toooooooooooo

toooooooooooo

or long curly snakes

to make up your own snakes and ladders tunes.

# Go tell Aunt Nancy

American folk song

# Green and white

# This is how I slip and slide

This is how I slip and slide.

On the glas-sy ice I ride.

I'm a four-beat note

# Three gentlemen

Three gen - tle - men to the wood did go,

Just as a phea - sant be - gan to crow, At -

- choum! At - choum! At - choum!

Traditional French

16

# Three sad seals

17

# Praise God from whom all blessings flow

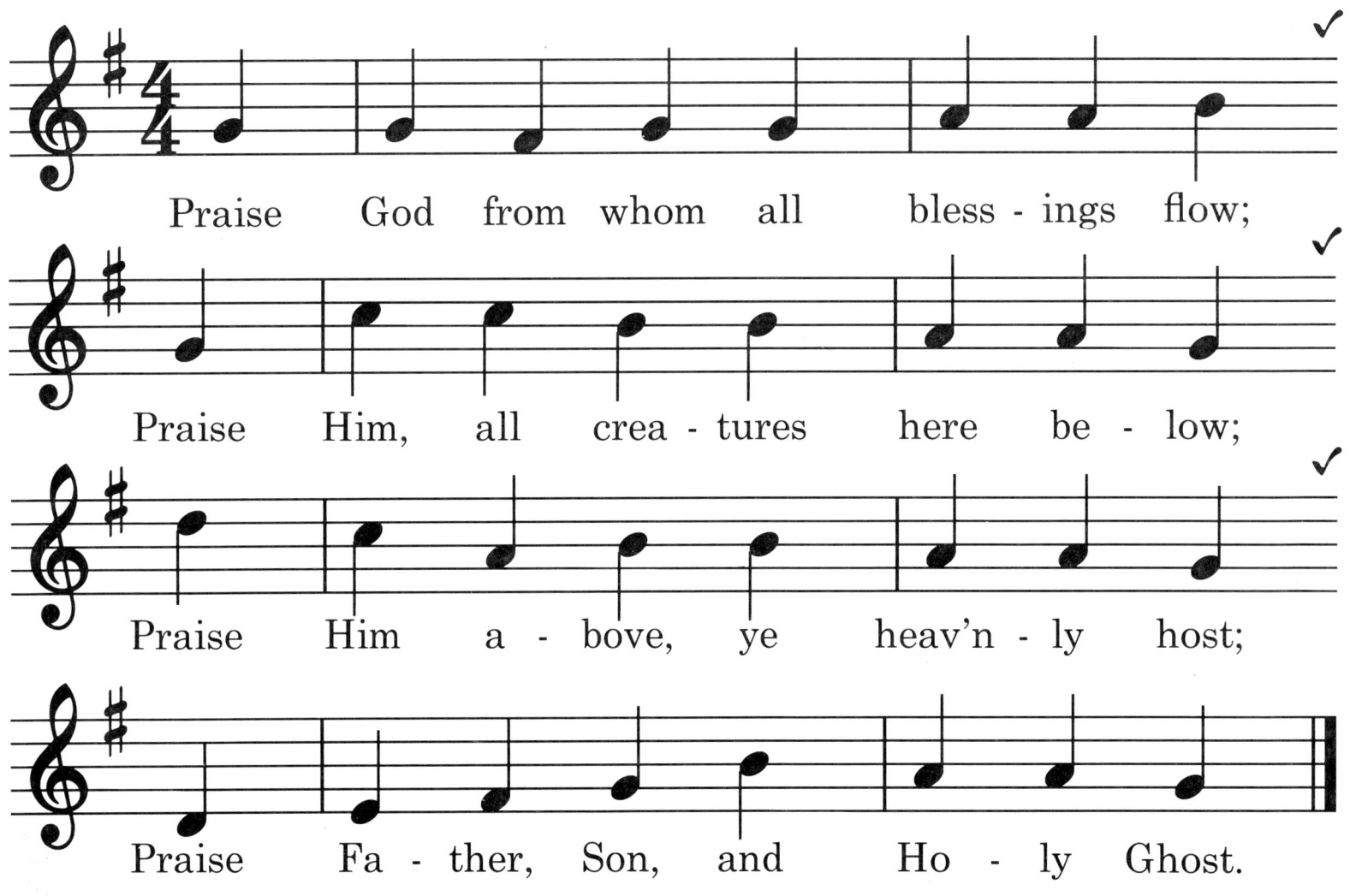

Praise God from whom all bless - ings flow;

Praise Him, all crea - tures here be - low;

Praise Him a - bove, ye heav'n - ly host;

Praise Fa - ther, Son, and Ho - ly Ghost.

'Tallis's Canon'

# Tickety, tackety, tickety tack

# C♯´

C sharp sounds a half-step higher than C. To play top C♯, finger the note A but lift off the thumb at the back, like this:

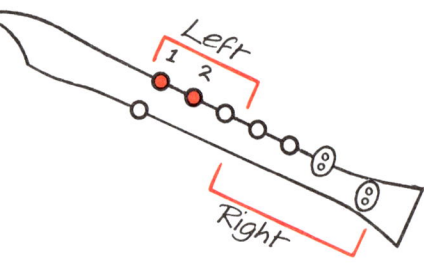

To write C sharp, put a sharp sign in front of C, like this:

# Thumb Twister Mix

A tongue twister is tricky to say.
A thumb twister might be tricky to play.
These thumb twisters mix the notes
A and C´ (thumb-hole closed) with
C♯´ and D´ (thumb-hole open).

As with tongue twisters, practise them
again and again until you can play them well.

This thumb twister changes time as well:

I'm C natural or just plain C

Can you make up some more thumb twisters with these notes?

# Sharp Ahead!

Look out!    Look out!    Keep  a  good    look out,

For there's a        sharp        a - head.

# Key of D

Tunes which use C♯ often end on D. They are in the key of D.
To show this, add C♯ to the key signature, like this:

Now there are two sharps in the key signature

## Chocker whacker, chocker whacker, great big ball

I tell you that every C is sharp

# One little brown bird

Try adding this second part to the tune above.
Except in one place the rhythm is the same.
Can you see where that is?

# Dickory Dock

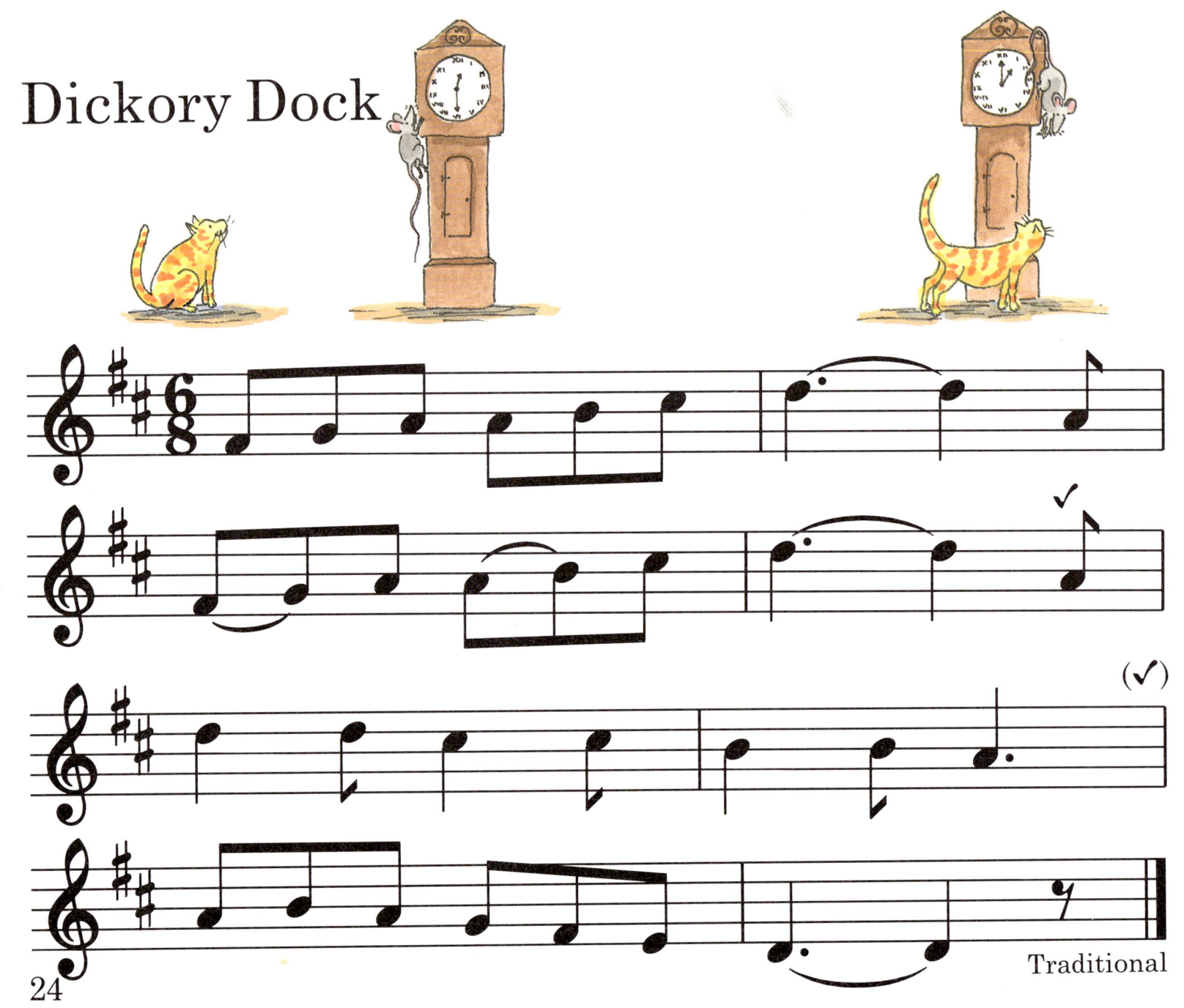

Traditional

24